ROLL IT, SLICE IT, MASH IT, DICE IT!

SUPER YUMMY RECIPES FOR KIDS

LISA O'DRISCOLL

CASTLE POINT BOOKS
NEW YORK

CONTENTS

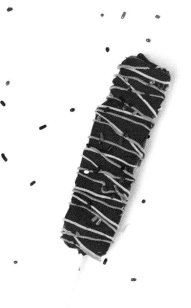

YOU CAN ROCK THE KITCHEN

Have you always wanted to surprise your best friend with amazing birthday cupcakes made from scratch? Cook a fun and delicious breakfast for your sleepover buddies? Impress everyone at your lunch table with what's in the bag? Create an after-school snack you'll want to show off on social? Even come to your family's rescue at dinnertime with an easy meal everyone will ask for again and again? You can do it all, with the step-by-step recipes in this cookbook!

Every recipe will help you master kitchen skills and find ways to make your cooking creations all your own. Even if you're sort of comfortable in the kitchen already, the creative ideas in these pages will help take you—and the food you make—to a whole new level. Most of all, you'll have fun reimagining food and dreaming up new recipes based on what you learn. Who knows, you could be a famous chef, cookbook author, or cooking show host someday! No matter what your future holds, you'll enjoy time in the kitchen and all the yummy creations you can make. The best part is that you now have full permission to play with your food!

TOP TIPS FOR GETTING STARTED

1. Choose a recipe. Sure, you can choose by type of dish—breakfast versus dessert. Or you can use the index (starting on page 172) to look for a featured

DECODING THE SYMBOLS

The recipes in this cookbook have two "codes" that also help you make a selection:

• • • •

Forks represent the difficulty level of the recipe.

Beginner

Intermediate

Advanced
(You will definitely need an adult to help you.)

• • • •

Dietary categories help you find what you need.

food you want to include. (Chocolate, anyone? Or maybe cheese, please?) Also, keep in mind how much time you have to spend in the kitchen. Every recipe lets you know right at the top how much time it takes to prepare and how much time it takes to cook.

2. Make a clean start. Be sure your kitchen counter and equipment are clean and ready to use. Don't forget to wash your hands.

3. Do the prep. You may be tempted to go straight for the delicious reward! But taking just a minute to get all the prep work done first helps everything go smoothly and gives you the best results. Make sure that you always start with reading over the recipe once to get an idea of what you need, how long it will take, and how to approach the recipe.

A secret that cooking pros live by: *mise en place*, which is a fancy French phrase that means "everything in its place." Get all the ingredients right in front of you, measured out and ready to go. This way, you won't find yourself wondering halfway through making a batch of cookies if you remembered to add the sugar or, worse, discovering that the sugar canister is completely empty.

4. Keep it safe. Accidents are most likely to happen when we are rushing or not paying attention. The best safety step you can take is also the easiest: slow down and enjoy what you're doing in the kitchen. While you're having fun:

- Wash your hands and clean up your space anytime you touch raw eggs or raw meat.
- Make sure your food is clean before including it in your recipe. (So, wash fruits and vegetables.)
- Keep handles turned inward when using a skillet on the stove top.
- Hold knives and scissors properly, making sure your fingers are guarded when chopping food.
- Stay near the stove when it is on.
- Wear oven mitts when handling hot food and cookware.
- Ask for help from an adult if something feels too difficult or advanced.
- Clean up your workstation when your recipe is complete.

5. Keep it fun! If something doesn't turn out exactly as you had hoped, don't be too hard on yourself. Look back over the steps in the recipe, using your detective skills to figure out what happened. Remember that the more you keep at it, the better you'll get. Almost every cook—from kid to pro—has an oopsie story. (In fact, a bunch of our favorite foods—Popsicles, ice cream cones, and potato chips—were invented by accident!) The goal is to use your creativity in the kitchen and love what you are doing.

BEYOND-BASIC BREAKFASTS

Yum, you've created a monster! Will you devour it for breakfast or dessert?

CRESCENT ROLL MONSTERS

MAKES
8 monsters
PREP TIME:
20 minutes
COOK TIME:
12-14 minutes

Monsters don't have to be scary. In fact, these little guys are actually pretty sweet, filled with fruit and cream cheese and topped with confectioners' sugar. The only trouble they will bring you is whether to enjoy them for breakfast or dessert!

INGREDIENTS

15 strawberries

²/₃ cup blueberries

4 ounces cream cheese

1 tube (8 count) refrigerated crescent rolls

2 tablespoons confectioners' sugar

EQUIPMENT

Baking sheet

Cooking spray

Cutting board

Paring knife

Toothpicks

Icing bag with small tip (optional)

Sifter

1. Preheat the oven to 375°F. Coat a baking sheet with nonstick cooking spray.

2. On a cutting board, slice the tops off the strawberries. Cut 12 of the strawberries in half. Slice the remaining three for the monster tongues.

3. Use a toothpick to make small holes through the center of 16 blueberries. With your fingers or an icing bag fitted with a small tip, fill the holes with cream cheese and set aside.

TIPS

Place paper towels or a baking sheet underneath the cooling rack to catch any runoff as the glaze sets.

1. Preheat the oven to 350°F. Coat a mini doughnut pan with nonstick cooking spray.

2. **To make the doughnuts:** In a large bowl or bowl of a stand mixer, mix the cake mix, eggs, water, and oil until well combined.

3. Fill each doughnut cavity three-quarters full with batter.

4. Add 3 to 5 blueberries to the batter of each doughnut. (You can mix the blueberries right into the batter too, but they'll be more evenly distributed if you add them to the doughnut pan.)

5. Bake for 8 to 10 minutes, or until a toothpick inserted into a doughnut comes out clean.

6. Let the doughnuts cool for 15 minutes.

7. **To make the glaze:** In a medium bowl, whisk the confectioners' sugar, milk, and vanilla, then add the blue food coloring to get the desired color.

8. Dip the cooled doughnuts into the glaze, then place the doughnuts on a cooling rack to set before serving.

ROLL IT, SLICE IT, MASH IT, DICE IT!

ICED TOASTER TARTS

MAKES
4 tarts
PREP TIME:
15 minutes
COOK TIME:
12-14 minutes

Think outside the cardboard box! Take one bite of these toaster tarts and you'll never want store-bought again. You can choose your favorite filling and icing to match for a festive breakfast that's fun to make and decorate and delicious to eat.

NUT FREE

VEGE-TARIAN

TOASTER TARTS INGREDIENTS

1 tablespoon flour

2 refrigerated piecrusts (1 box)

½ cup strawberry preserves

1 egg white

ICING INGREDIENTS

1½ tablespoons milk

½ cup confectioners' sugar

Pink food coloring

Sprinkles

EQUIPMENT

Baking sheet

Cooking spray

Large cutting board

Knife

Spoon

Pastry brush

Fork

Small mixing bowl

1. Preheat the oven to 400°F. Coat a baking sheet with nonstick cooking spray.

2. **To make the tarts:** Sprinkle the flour over a large cutting board. Unroll one piecrust and cut it into four rectangles. Place the rectangles on the baking sheet.

TIPS

To separate the egg yolk from the white, have two small bowls ready. Crack the egg as close as you can to the middle. Over one of the bowls, gently pry the egg apart, letting the yolk settle in the bottom half of the shell. Some egg white will run over the side and into the bowl. To catch the rest, transfer the egg yolk back and forth between the eggshell halves, letting as much egg white as you can drip into the bowl below. The yolk can then be placed in the other bowl and saved for another use.

If the icing is too thin, add more confectioners' sugar. If it's too thick, add a little more milk until you get the texture you want.

3. Drop 2 tablespoons of strawberry preserves onto the center of each pastry rectangle. Spread the preserves but leave room at the edges.

4. Using a pastry brush, spread some egg white around the edges of the pastry rectangles. (This helps seal the edges so the filling won't seep out.)

5. Return to the cutting board, unroll the second piecrust and cut it into four rectangles. Place these on top of the first set of rectangles and seal by pushing a fork into the dough around every edge of the tarts.

6. Use the fork to gently poke three or four sets of holes in the top of each pastry, then brush the tops with the remaining egg white.

7. Bake for 12 to 14 minutes, or until the tops of the tarts turn golden brown. Remove from the oven and allow to cool for about 5 minutes.

8. **To make the icing:** In a small bowl, mix the milk, confectioners' sugar, and a drop of pink food coloring.

9. After the toaster tarts have cooled, spread the icing over the top and add sprinkles.

TRIPLE-BERRY BREAKFAST SMOOTHIE

MAKES
1 smoothie

PREP TIME:
5 minutes

EGG FREE

NUT FREE

GLUTEN FREE

VEGE-TARIAN

Healthy eating (or sipping) doesn't have to be boring. With fresh strawberries, blueberries, and raspberries, this sweet wake-up call with a straw will get you energized for the day ahead in just 5 minutes.

INGREDIENTS

⅓ cup strawberries

¼ cup blueberries

¼ cup raspberries

½ cup vanilla yogurt

½ cup ice

EQUIPMENT

Paring knife or strawberry huller

Blender

Glass

Straw

1. Use a paring knife or strawberry huller to remove the stem and leaves from the strawberries.

2. Combine the berries, yogurt, and ice in a blender and blend until smooth.

3. Pour into a glass, add a fun straw, and enjoy.

RISE-AND-SHINE PIZZA

MAKES
8 slices
PREP TIME:
10 minutes
COOK TIME:
15 minutes

NUT
FREE

Who says you can't have pizza for breakfast? This recipe takes favorite breakfast ingredients and puts them together on a crispy pizza crust. It's easy to add or subtract toppings to your liking, just like ordering from your favorite pizza place.

INGREDIENTS

1 refrigerated pizza crust

4 eggs

1 tablespoon milk

½ tablespoon butter or olive oil

¼ cup ground breakfast sausage

½ cup onion slices

1¼ cups shredded cheddar cheese, divided

Salt and black pepper to taste

EQUIPMENT

Baking sheet

Cooking spray

Medium mixing bowl

Whisk

Medium nonstick skillet

Spatula

Small plate or bowl

Pizza cutter

1. Preheat the oven to 400°F. Coat a baking sheet with nonstick cooking spray.

2. Place the pizza crust on the baking sheet, using your fingers to spread it into a square. It doesn't need to reach the edges; you just want to thin it out a little.

3. Precook the crust for 8 minutes.

1. Coat a 9 x 13-inch baking dish with nonstick cooking spray.

2. **To make the French toast:** In a large bowl, combine the bread cubes, apple pie filling, brown sugar, and cinnamon. Spread the mixture evenly across the baking dish.

3. In a medium bowl, combine the eggs, milk, and vanilla. Pour the egg mixture over the bread mixture, covering every piece and pushing the bread down into the egg mix as needed to get it wet.

4. Cover with plastic wrap and refrigerate overnight.

5. **To make the pecan topping:** Cut the butter into small pieces and mix with the pecans, brown sugar, and cinnamon. Store in an airtight container.

6. In the morning, preheat the oven to 350°F.

7. Sprinkle the pecan topping over the casserole and bake for 35 minutes.

8. **Extras:** Use a sifter to add confectioners' sugar. Top with maple syrup and whipped cream (if using).

Make It Your Way: Not crazy for nuts? Simply leave out the pecans.

Add edible flowers made with berries and celery!

BREAKFAST BUTTERFLY

Make breakfast rise above a basic bowl of cereal with this butterfly that's as much fun to create as it is to eat! Starting your day with yogurt, granola, and superfood berries will keep your energy going strong so you soar.

MAKES
1 butterfly
PREP TIME:
5 minutes

INGREDIENTS

1 banana

⅓ cup vanilla yogurt

⅓ cup granola

½ cup raspberries and blackberries

EQUIPMENT

Knife

Plate

Spoon

1. Cut the banana in half and place it on a plate, flat sides up with "wings" curved out.

2. Spoon some yogurt over the middle of the butterfly, with a smaller spoonful at the top to make the head.

3. Add the granola in a vertical line to make the body of the butterfly. Add another spoonful for the head, then create two small lines for the antennae.

4. Separate one blackberry and use the pieces to finish the antennae and to make the eyes.

5. Top the banana halves with the raspberries and remaining blackberries.

SUNSHINE SCRAMBLE QUESADILLAS

MAKES
2 servings
PREP TIME:
10 minutes
COOK TIME:
15 minutes

NUT FREE

Wake up your breakfast routine with a cheesy egg quesadilla for breakfast! Just take a tortilla and cover it with some of your favorite breakfast foods. Seal all the yum in with another tortilla on top, cook for a few more minutes, and your new favorite breakfast is ready for slicing and serving.

INGREDIENTS

⅓ cup ground breakfast sausage

⅓ cup sliced mushrooms

2 eggs

½ tablespoon milk

½ tablespoon butter

2 6-inch flour tortillas

¼ cup shredded cheddar cheese

EQUIPMENT

Large skillet

Small mixing bowl

Whisk

Spatula

Knife or pizza cutter

1. In a large skillet over medium heat, sauté the sausage and mushrooms until cooked through, about 3 minutes. Remove from the skillet and set aside.

2. Crack the eggs into a small bowl and whisk with the milk until well beaten.

3. Pour the egg and milk mixture into the skillet, and scramble them in the skillet over medium heat until the eggs are set. Remove from the skillet and set aside.

4. Add the butter to the skillet over medium heat. Add one tortilla and top with half the cheddar cheese and all of the eggs, sausage, and mushrooms. Finish with the remaining cheddar. Top with the second tortilla.

5. Cook on both sides, turning with a spatula, until the cheese is melted and the tortillas turn golden brown. Cut in half and share with someone you love.

Make It Your Way: To make just one serving, cut the amount of sausage, mushrooms, eggs, and cheese in half, then place all the toppings on one side of the tortilla and fold over.

PEACH OVERNIGHT OAT MAGIC

MAKES
2 servings
PREP TIME:
5 minutes
ADDITIONAL
TIME:
Overnight

Want to wake up to a breakfast ready and waiting? Whip up these peach oats the night before, pop them in the fridge, and you're good to go. Since this recipe makes two servings, you'll even have some to share!

EGG FREE

NUT FREE

VEGE-TARIAN

INGREDIENTS

½ cup vanilla Greek yogurt

½ cup milk

½ cup old-fashioned oats

1½ tablespoons honey

¾ cup diced peaches

EQUIPMENT

Large mason jar with lid or other airtight container

Spoon

1. In a large mason jar, mix the yogurt, milk, oats, honey, and most of the peaches. Place the remaining peaches on top of the mixture.

2. Cover the jar or container with the lid and refrigerate overnight.

3. Divide into two servings and enjoy.

Make It Your Way: These overnight oats can be made with any fruit you like! Try blueberries, strawberries, or other favorites.

MINI EGG AND BACON MUFFINS

You've got a life to live, and you need breakfast to fuel it. These muffins are perfect to make ahead, reheat, and take on the go.

MAKES
12 mini muffins
PREP TIME:
10 minutes
COOK TIME:
20 minutes

NUT FREE

GLUTEN FREE

INGREDIENTS

⅓ cup frozen hash browns

3 eggs

2 tablespoons milk

⅓ cup bacon crumbles

⅓ cup shredded cheddar cheese

Extra cheese, bacon, and chopped fresh parsley, for garnish (optional)

EQUIPMENT

Mini muffin tin

Cooking spray

Spoon

Medium mixing bowl

Whisk

1. Preheat the oven to 350°F. Coat a mini muffin tin with nonstick cooking spray.

2. Line the bottom of each muffin cup with hash browns.

3. Crack the eggs into a medium bowl and whisk with the milk until well beaten. Add the bacon and cheddar cheese.

4. Spoon the egg mixture over the hash browns. Bake for 20 minutes.

5. Garnish with extra cheese, bacon, and parsley (if using).

LEVEL-UP LUNCHES

MAC AND CHEESE BITES

MAKES
24 bites
PREP TIME:
20 minutes
COOK TIME:
15 minutes

These cheesy bites may be little but they're packed full of flavor! Try a fun take on a favorite lunch that makes it totally acceptable to eat mac and cheese with your hands.

INGREDIENTS

1 cup uncooked elbow macaroni

2 tablespoons unsalted butter

2 tablespoons all-purpose flour

1¼ cups milk

2 cups shredded cheddar cheese

¾ cup cubed ham

Salt and black pepper to taste

1 egg, slightly beaten

Extra cheese and fresh parsley, for garnish (optional)

EQUIPMENT

2 mini muffin tins

Cooking spray

Colander

Medium saucepan

Whisk

Large mixing bowl

Spoon

1. Preheat the oven to 425°F. Coat two mini muffin tins with nonstick cooking spray.

2. Cook the pasta according to package directions; drain in a colander and set aside.

3. Melt the butter in a medium saucepan over medium heat. Whisk in the flour.

TIPS

Make this recipe even easier by using precooked bacon.

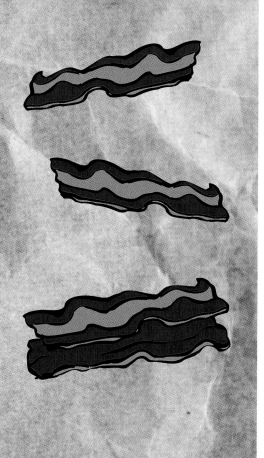

4. Push a piece of chicken onto a skewer, followed by a cube of cheese, and ⅓ slice of bacon. Repeat two more times. Do the same with the remaining skewers. Each will have three pieces of chicken, cheese, and bacon.

5. Dip into your favorite sauce and enjoy.

Make It Your Way: Get creative with your skewer combinations! Try adding pineapple chunks or apple slices.

TURKEY AND CHEESE CRESCENT ROLLS

MAKES
8 rolls
PREP TIME:
5 minutes
COOK TIME:
12 minutes

EGG FREE

NUT FREE

You can take sandwiches from ordinary to amazing in minutes, with just three ingredients! Impress everyone with warm turkey and melted cheese inside a buttery, melt-in-your-mouth crescent roll. Switch up the meat and cheese selection, or add a tasty dressing you like.

INGREDIENTS

1 tube (8 count) refrigerated crescent rolls

16 thin slices deli turkey

4 slices Swiss cheese, cut in half

EQUIPMENT

Baking sheet

Cooking spray

Cutting board

1. Preheat the oven to 375°F. Coat a baking sheet with nonstick cooking spray.

2. Open the crescent tube and unroll the dough on a cutting board. Separate the crescents at the seams.

3. Place two slices of turkey on each crescent, then top with half a slice of Swiss cheese. Starting with the wide end, roll the crescents and place them on the baking sheet. (You should end up with the narrow end lying over the top of the wide end.)

4. Bake for 12 minutes, or until golden brown.

SOUTHWEST LETTUCE WRAPS

MAKES
4 wraps

PREP TIME:
10 minutes

COOK TIME:
10 minutes

EGG FREE

GLUTEN FREE

NUT FREE

Tortillas aren't the only fun holders you can fill with deliciousness. Leaves of romaine lettuce add a little crunch and big nutrition to your lunch. It's easy to customize the fillings and toppings to just what you like.

INGREDIENTS

2 cups diced chicken

2 teaspoons fajita seasoning

1 tablespoon olive oil

4 whole romaine lettuce leaves

¼ cup black beans

¼ cup canned corn

½ cup diced tomatoes

½ cup shredded cheddar cheese

4 tablespoons ranch dressing

EQUIPMENT

Medium mixing bowl

Large skillet

Wooden spoon or spatula

Paper towel

Spoon

1. In a medium bowl, combine the chicken and fajita seasoning until all the pieces are evenly covered.

2. Add the olive oil to a large skillet over medium heat. Add the chicken and sauté, stirring occasionally, until cooked through. Remove from the heat and set aside.

TORTILLA PIZZAS

MAKES
2 pizzas
PREP TIME:
10 minutes
COOK TIME:
5-7 minutes

Pizza is pretty much perfect for every meal! Using a tortilla as the base makes it super-easy too. Just add your favorite toppings, bake, and eat.

INGREDIENTS

2 6-inch flour tortillas

4 tablespoons pizza sauce

1 cup shredded mozzarella cheese

½ teaspoon Italian seasoning

10 pepperoni slices

EQUIPMENT

Baking sheet

Cooking spray

Pastry brush

1. Preheat the oven to 400°F. Coat a baking sheet with cooking spray.

2. Place the tortillas on the baking sheet. Using a pastry brush, spread the pizza sauce on the tortillas.

3. Scatter the mozzarella cheese over the sauce, then sprinkle the Italian seasoning over the top. Add the pepperoni slices.

4. Bake for 5 to 7 minutes, or until the cheese is melted.

Give lunch a fun twist!

HAM AND CHEESE PINWHEELS

MAKES
10 pinwheels
PREP TIME:
5 minutes

EGG
FREE

NUT
FREE

These bite-size wraps look gourmet but are easy to make with just five simple ingredients—or any swaps you choose to make. If you're taking them on the go, consider bringing extras for friends who'll try to talk you into trading.

INGREDIENTS

2 6-inch flour tortillas

2 tablespoons cream cheese

2 slices cheddar cheese

8 thin slices deli ham

1 tablespoon Dijon mustard

EQUIPMENT

Cutting board

Knife

Toothpicks

1. Lay the tortillas flat on a cutting board and spread the cream cheese down the middle of each.

2. Cut the cheddar slices in half and place two each on top of the cream cheese.

3. Add four slices of ham to each tortilla, then spread with the mustard.

4. Roll the tortillas tightly and cut each into five slices, using toothpicks to keep the pinwheels from unrolling.

STACK 'EM HIGH CLUB SANDWICHES

MAKES
2 sandwiches
PREP TIME:
10 minutes

Pile on all the club sandwich classics—lightly toasted bread, flavorful meats and cheese, and mayo—to create your masterpiece. Then hide...because everyone's going to want a bite!

INGREDIENTS

6 slices bread

6 thins slices deli turkey

4 slices cheddar cheese

2 slices tomato

6 thin slices deli ham

2 large lettuce leaves

2 tablespoons mayonnaise

EQUIPMENT

Toaster

Knife

Toothpick

1. Toast the bread lightly in a toaster; let cool slightly.

2. Top each of two bread slices with three turkey slices, a cheese slice, and a tomato slice.

3. Add another bread slice to each sandwich, then top each with three ham slices, a cheese slice, and a lettuce leaf.

4. Spread the mayonnaise across the remaining two pieces of bread and place them on top of the sandwiches. Secure in place with a toothpick.

GRILLED TUNA MELTS

It's a masterful mash-up of two lunch favorites: tuna meets grilled cheese in perfect harmony. Made from ingredients probably in your kitchen right now, it's ready to enjoy in no time.

MAKES
2 sandwiches

PREP TIME:
10 minutes

COOK TIME:
4-6 minutes

NUT
FREE

INGREDIENTS

1 can tuna, packed in water

2 tablespoons mayonnaise

1 tablespoon chopped celery

Salt and black pepper to taste

2 tablespoons butter

4 slices bread

2 slices Swiss cheese

EQUIPMENT

Can opener

Small mixing bowl

Spoon

Knife

Large skillet

Spatula

1. Drain the tuna and transfer to a small bowl. Stir in the mayonnaise, celery, salt, and pepper. Set aside.

2. Butter one side of each bread slice.

3. In a large skillet over medium heat, place two of the bread slices butter side down. Divide the tuna mixture onto each slice, then top with a slice of Swiss cheese. Finish each sandwich with the second slice of bread, butter side up.

4. Cook for 2 to 3 minutes, or until the bread begins to turn golden brown. (Lift it with a spatula to peek underneath.) Flip and cook on the other side for 2 to 3 minutes more. When both sides are golden, you're ready for lunch.

Make It Your Way: Reimagine your melt by substituting canned chicken for the tuna and diced apple or dried cranberries for the celery.

TIPS

Easily drain your tuna by opening the can and pushing the lid down into the tuna. The juice will rise to the top and you can easily pour it into the sink while keeping the tuna in the can.

FUN FAMILY DINNERS

Add a little adventure to your next taco dinner!

TACO BOATS

Help your family cruise into dinnertime with a fun twist on tacos. With a crunchy sail and a boat filled with delicious cargo, these are way too good to save for just Tuesdays.

MAKES
12 boats
PREP TIME:
20 minutes
COOK TIME:
12 minutes

EGG
FREE

NUT
FREE

INGREDIENTS

12 mini soft tortilla bowls

1 pound 80 or 85% lean ground beef

1 package taco seasoning

¾ cup water

¼ cup shredded lettuce

½ cup diced tomatoes

½ cup cheddar cheese

¼ cup taco sauce

12 lettuce leaves for sails

EQUIPMENT

Baking sheet

Large skillet

Spoon (silicone or wooden, for stirring)

Knife or kitchen scissors

12 wooden skewers

1. Preheat the oven to 350°F.

2. Place the tortilla bowls on a baking sheet and bake for 5 minutes, or until golden.

3. In a large skillet over medium heat, brown the ground beef. Drain and return to the skillet.

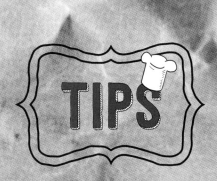

TIPS

Look for tortilla bowls in your grocery store's international section.

Iceberg lettuce works best for the sails.

If you're having trouble keeping the skewers upright, poke the bottom of the skewer through a tomato piece to anchor it.

4. Stir in the taco seasoning and water. Bring to a boil, then simmer for 5 minutes, or until the sauce thickens.

5. Fill the bowls with the meat mixture, then add the lettuce, tomatoes, and cheese. Drizzle the taco sauce over the top.

6. Cut four large lettuce leaves into triangles and push the wooden skewers through one side to create sails. Stand the sails up in the tortilla bowls before serving.

Make It Your Way: Try making the boat prep a family affair. Bake the bowls and cook the meat, then create a toppings bar for each person to race to a customized, fabulous-tasting finish.

BACON CHEESEBURGER CASSEROLE

MAKES
8-10 servings

PREP TIME:
15 minutes

COOK TIME:
20 minutes

NUT FREE

Loaded with bacon and cheddar, this dinner is sure to become a family favorite. And it tastes like much more work is involved than it actually is! Chances are, you'll have some leftovers for a winning repeat dinner the next day too.

INGREDIENTS

1½ cups uncooked egg noodles

10 slices bacon

1 pound 80 or 85% lean ground beef

½ cup chopped onion

1 can (14.5 ounces) diced tomatoes, drained

¼ cup ketchup

2 tablespoons Worcestershire sauce

1 teaspoon minced garlic

1 teaspoon salt

1 teaspoon black pepper

2 cups shredded cheddar cheese

EQUIPMENT

Large pot

Colander

Paper towels

Microwave-safe plate

Large skillet

Spoon (silicone or wooden, for stirring)

9 x 13-inch baking dish

1. Preheat the oven to 375°F.

2. In a large pot, boil the noodles according to package directions. Drain in a colander; set aside.

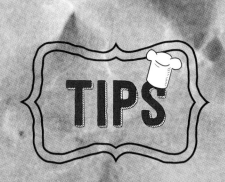

TIPS

Cooking bacon can be messy! To make it easier, use ¾ cup of store-bought bacon crumbles in this recipe.

3. Place a paper towel on a microwave-safe plate and lay five slices of bacon on top. Cover with a second paper towel and microwave for 3 to 4 minutes, until crispy. Repeat with the remaining bacon slices; set aside to cool.

4. In a large skillet, brown the ground beef. Drain and transfer to a 9 x 13-inch baking dish.

5. With clean hands, crumble the bacon.

6. Stir the bacon, onion, tomatoes, ketchup, Worcestershire sauce, garlic, salt, and pepper into the beef.

7. Add the noodles and cheddar cheese to the beef mixture and mix well.

8. Bake for 10 minutes, or until the cheese melts. Serve hot.

Make It Your Way: For a healthier version, substitute ground turkey breast for the beef.

ROLL IT, SLICE IT, MASH IT, DICE IT!

MINI MEAT LOAVES

MAKES
12 loaves
PREP TIME:
15 minutes
COOK TIME:
25-30 minutes

There is a bit of magic inside these meat loaves: melty cheddar cheese. Although they're mini in size, their taste comes up big. Serve with a salad for a complete dinner your family will love.

NUT
FREE

INGREDIENTS

2 pounds 80 or 85% lean ground beef

½ small white onion, chopped

½ tablespoon minced garlic

2 tablespoons Worcestershire sauce

⅔ cup Italian-style bread crumbs

1 egg, slightly beaten

½ cup shredded cheddar cheese

¾ cup ketchup

2 tablespoons brown sugar

EQUIPMENT

Large mixing bowl

Cooking spray

Muffin tin

Small mixing bowl

Spoon

Baking sheet

Meat thermometer

1. Preheat the oven to 400°F.

2. In a large bowl, combine the ground beef, onion, garlic, Worcestershire sauce, bread crumbs, and egg.
Use your hands to mix thoroughly.

3. Coat the muffin tin with cooking spray, then divide the meat loaf mixture evenly among the 12 muffin tin compartments.

4. Use your finger to make an indentation two-thirds of the way down the middle of each meat loaf. Fill the indentation almost to the top with the cheddar cheese, then close the opening by pushing the meat loaf together at the top.

5. In a small bowl, mix the ketchup and brown sugar together, then spoon over the top of each meat loaf.

6. Place the muffin tin on a baking sheet and bake for 25 to 30 minutes, or until a meat thermometer inserted in the center of a loaf reads 160°F.

Make It Your Way: Make a healthier version of these mini meat loaves by using ground turkey breast instead of beef.

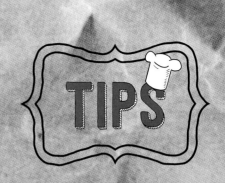

TIPS

If you don't want to get your hands dirty (even though that's the fun part), combine the ingredients in a gallon-size plastic storage bag and knead until well blended.

Get on a roll with this delicious dinner!

BARBECUE CHICKEN SLIDERS

MAKES
12 sliders
PREP TIME:
15 minutes
COOK TIME:
8-10 minutes

NUT FREE

Sensational sliders will gather everyone to the dinner table quickly. Don't have a big family? These sandwiches are so full of flavor, dripping with barbecue sauce and melted cheese, that the leftovers taste just as good the next day.

INGREDIENTS

2 cups shredded cooked chicken

¾ cup barbecue sauce

⅓ cup chopped red onion

12 Hawaiian rolls

3 slices cheddar cheese

1 tablespoon butter, melted

1 teaspoon chopped fresh parsley

EQUIPMENT

Baking sheet

Cooking spray

Large mixing bowl

Spoon

Small bowl

Pastry brush

1. Preheat the oven to 350°F. Coat a baking sheet with nonstick cooking spray.

2. In a large bowl, combine the shredded chicken, barbecue sauce, and red onion.

3. Place the bottom halves of the Hawaiian rolls on the baking sheet.

TIPS

Rotisserie chicken works great in this recipe. Just pull the meat apart with two forks to shred.

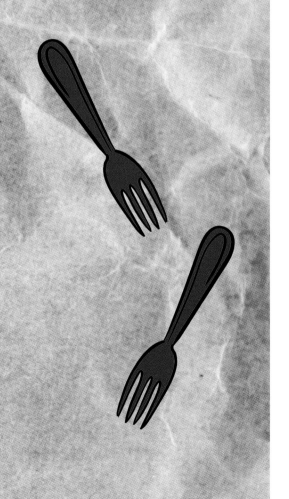

4. Spoon the chicken mixture onto each roll.

5. Cut each cheese slice into four squares and add one piece to each slider.

6. Add the top halves of the rolls.

7. In a small bowl, mix the butter and parsley together. Use a pastry brush to spread the mixture onto the tops of the rolls.

8. Cover the sliders loosely with foil and bake for 8 to 10 minutes, or until the cheese is melted. Serve warm.

POTATO CHIP-CRUSTED CHICKEN DRUMSTICKS

MAKES
8 drumsticks
PREP TIME:
15 minutes
COOK TIME:
30-35 minutes

GLUTEN FREE

NUT FREE

Shhh, potato chips are the secret ingredient that makes these drumsticks so tasty and crispy. And they're amazingly fun to crush with a rolling pin. Had a rough day? Offer to make this chicken dinner!

INGREDIENTS

2 cups potato chips

2 eggs, lightly beaten

¼ teaspoon salt

¼ teaspoon black pepper

8 chicken drumsticks

EQUIPMENT

Baking rack

Baking sheet

Gallon-size food storage bag

Rolling pin

Large shallow bowl

Small shallow bowl

Whisk or fork

Meat thermometer

1. Preheat the oven to 400°F.
Set a baking rack inside a baking sheet.

2. Place the potato chips in a gallon-size food storage bag. Roll over the bag with a rolling pin to crush the chips. Empty the chips into a large shallow bowl and set aside.

3. Break the eggs into a small shallow bowl and beat with a whisk or fork. Add the salt and black pepper.

4. One at a time, dip the drumsticks into the egg mixture, then roll in the crushed potato chips.

5. Place the drumsticks on the baking rack and bake for 30 to 35 minutes, or until a meat thermometer registers 165°F. (Thicker pieces will need more time.)

Make It Your Way: Try replacing the chips with buttery crackers or cornflake cereal.

PRETZEL DOGS

Want to give your taste buds a delicious present? Try this hot dog wrapped in a pretzel! Just whip up a batch of pretzel dough, wrap it around a juicy hot dog, and bake for a new dinner twist.

MAKES
8 dogs
PREP TIME:
20 minutes
COOK TIME:
10-12 minutes
ADDITIONAL TIME:
10 minutes

EGG FREE

NUT FREE

INGREDIENTS

¼ cup warm water

1 tablespoon active dry yeast

½ cup milk

1 tablespoon granulated sugar

½ teaspoon salt

2 cups all-purpose flour
(plus 1 tablespoon to sprinkle
on cutting board)

8 hot dogs

⅔ cup baking soda

3 tablespoons butter, melted

1 tablespoon kosher salt

EQUIPMENT

Baking sheet

Parchment paper

Cooking spray

Large mixing bowl

Spoon

Large cutting board
(or you can use the counter)

Large pot

Slotted spoon

Pastry brush

1. Line a baking sheet with parchment paper and coat lightly with nonstick cooking spray.

2. In a large bowl, combine the water and yeast. Stir in the milk, sugar, and ½ teaspoon of salt.

3. Add the 2 cups of flour and stir until it forms a dough.

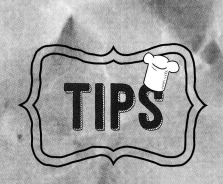

TIPS

If the dough gets too sticky while you're working with it, just add more flour to your hands or the cutting board.

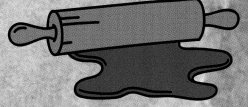

4. Sprinkle the extra 1 tablespoon of flour on a large cutting board or clean counter. Rub a little flour onto your hands too. Knead the dough, then let it sit for 10 minutes.

5. Roll the dough into eight long, ropelike pieces.

6. Wrap the dough around each hot dog, leaving just a little of the hot dog poking out at each end. Tuck the end of the dough underneath and give it a little pinch to seal it.

7. Preheat the oven to 450°F.

8. Fill a large pot with water. Add the baking soda and bring to a boil. One or two at a time, use a slotted spoon to gently drop the pretzel hot dogs into the boiling water for 30 seconds. Remove from the water and place on the baking sheet.

9. Using a pastry brush, coat the hot dogs with the melted butter, and sprinkle with the kosher salt.

10. Bake for 10 to 12 minutes, or until the pretzel dough turns golden brown.

HAWAIIAN CHICKEN AND RICE

MAKES
4 servings
PREP TIME:
15 minutes
COOK TIME:
10 minutes

NUT FREE

You don't need to travel to a tropical island to enjoy this delicious Hawaiian chicken and rice! Make the easy recipe any night of the week right in your family's kitchen. Start by marinating your chicken the night before, and your dinner will be even easier and more flavorful.

INGREDIENTS

1 cup uncooked rice

1 can (20 ounces) pineapple chunks, packed in juice

¼ cup brown sugar

¼ cup soy sauce

¼ cup honey barbecue sauce

1 tablespoon fresh ginger, chopped

1 teaspoon minced garlic

3 boneless, skinless chicken breasts, cut into bite-size pieces

1 green bell pepper, chopped

EQUIPMENT

Rice cooker or saucepan with lid

Can opener

Large mixing bowl

Wooden spoon

Large skillet

Meat thermometer

1. Prepare the rice according to package directions. Set aside, keeping warm.

2. Drain the pineapple, saving 2 tablespoons of the juice.

TIPS

If you have the extra time, place the chicken and sauce in a gallon-size storage bag and marinate overnight in the refrigerator. This allows the chicken to soak up all the extra flavor and makes for an even tastier dinner.

3. In a large bowl, combine the pineapple, juice, brown sugar, soy sauce, barbecue sauce, ginger, and garlic.

4. Stir in the chicken and bell pepper.

5. In a large skillet over medium heat, cook the chicken mixture for about 10 minutes, or until a meat thermometer registers 165°F when inserted in the chicken.

6. Serve the chicken over the rice.

CHICKEN POTPIES

MAKES
8 servings
PREP TIME:
20 minutes
COOK TIME:
35 minutes

You'll win the prize for best comfort food dinner with these pies! Using puff pastry keeps the prep simple.

NUT FREE

INGREDIENTS

½ tablespoon olive oil

½ onion, chopped

½ tablespoon minced garlic

½ teaspoon thyme

½ teaspoon salt

½ teaspoon black pepper

¼ cup all-purpose flour

1 cup chicken broth

1 cup milk

2 cups cooked chicken cut into bite-size pieces

2 cups frozen mixed vegetables

1 box puff pastry, thawed

1 egg, beaten

½ tablespoon chopped fresh parsley

EQUIPMENT

Large saucepan

Large spoon

Cutting board

Round cookie cutter

8 ramekins

Baking sheet

Sharp knife

Pastry brush

1. In a large saucepan over medium heat, add the olive oil and sauté the onion for about 5 minutes, or until it begins to look translucent. Stir in the garlic and cook for an additional minute.

2. Add the thyme, salt, and pepper, then stir in the flour and mix well.

TIPS

Instead of a cookie cutter, you can use a small bowl or another circular object. Just make sure that the diameter of the circle is slightly larger than the top of the ramekin.

If you don't have thyme, try using rosemary instead.

3. Pour in the broth and milk and bring to a simmer.

4. Add the chicken and frozen vegetables. Continue to simmer until the sauce thickens, stirring frequently. Remove from the heat and let cool for about 10 minutes.

5. Preheat the oven to 400°F.

6. Sprinkle a bit of flour (about a tablespoon or so) on a cutting board, then place the puff pastry on it. Use a round cookie cutter to cut out eight circles that are about ½ inch larger than each ramekin all around. Set aside.

7. Place the ramekins on a baking sheet and fill with the chicken and vegetable mixture.

8. Top each ramekin with a puff pastry circle. Use a sharp knife to make a small slit in the top of the pastry, then brush with the egg.

9. Bake for 20 minutes.

10. Garnish with the parsley, and let cool for a few minutes before serving.

Puff pastry to the dinner rescue!

TACO STUFFED PEPPERS

MAKES
4 peppers
PREP TIME:
15 minutes
COOK TIME:
30 minutes

EGG
FREE

NUT
FREE

You can combine two family favorites in one amazing dish! Simple twists on seasonings and toppings take classic stuffed peppers on a fun and flavorful trip across the border.

INGREDIENTS

4 medium green bell peppers

1 tablespoon olive oil

1 cup chopped onion

3 cloves garlic, minced

1 pound 80 to 85% lean ground beef

1 package taco seasoning

¾ cup water

1 cup diced tomatoes

1 cup shredded cheddar cheese, divided

Salsa and sour cream for topping

EQUIPMENT

Knife

Large skillet

Wooden spoon

8 x 8-inch glass baking dish

1. Preheat the oven to 375°F.

2. Cut the tops off the bell peppers and remove the seeds. Set aside.

3. In a large skillet over medium heat, add the olive oil and sauté the onion until translucent.

4. Stir in the garlic and ground beef and cook through. Drain.

5. Return the beef to the skillet and add the taco seasoning and water. Bring to a boil, then reduce the heat and let simmer for about 5 minutes, or until the mixture has thickened.

6. Remove from the heat, then stir in the tomatoes and ½ cup of the cheddar cheese.

7. Place the bell peppers in an 8 x 8-inch baking dish and stuff with the beef mixture. Bake for 15 minutes.

8. Take the peppers out of the oven, top with the remaining cheese, and bake for another 5 minutes, or until the cheese is melted and bubbling.

9. Let cool slightly and serve with salsa and sour cream.

Make It Your Way: For a healthier version, use ground turkey breast instead of ground beef.

TIPS

If your peppers fall over or tilt to one side, you can cut a little sliver from the bottom to even them out.

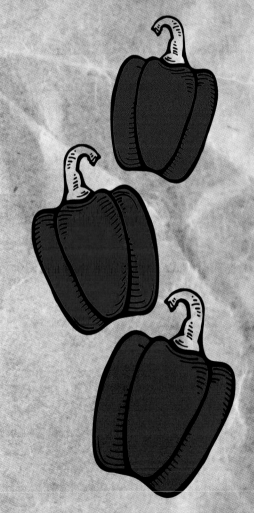

BEST-EVER CHICKEN NUGGETS

MAKES
6 servings
PREP TIME:
15 minutes
COOK TIME:
12 minutes

NUT
FREE

Everyone needs a go-to tender, crispy chicken nuggets recipe. Now you can cross it off your kitchen bucket list. After you try these, you'll never crave store-bought nuggets again! And they're so simple: just dip, roll, coat, bake, and gobble up.

INGREDIENTS

2 eggs

1½ cups panko bread crumbs

½ cup grated Parmesan cheese

1 tablespoon chopped fresh parsley

½ teaspoon salt

½ teaspoon black pepper

2 pounds boneless chicken tenders

3 tablespoons butter, melted

Barbecue sauce, ranch dressing, or honey mustard dressing, for dipping

EQUIPMENT

Baking sheet

Cooking spray

2 medium shallow bowls

Whisk or fork

Spoon

Knife

Meat thermometer

1. Preheat the oven to 450°F. Coat a baking sheet with nonstick cooking spray.

2. Crack the eggs into a medium shallow bowl and beat lightly with a whisk or fork.

SHAKE 'EM UP PORK CHOPS

MAKES
4 servings
PREP TIME:
15 minutes
COOK TIME:
25 minutes

EGG FREE

NUT FREE

Shake up dinner with this awesome pork chop recipe! Just put all your ingredients in a bag and toss until your chops are covered in deliciousness. Count down to a dinner that your family is going to love as the chops cook in the oven.

INGREDIENTS

1½ cups bread crumbs

1 teaspoon Italian seasoning

½ teaspoon garlic powder

½ teaspoon onion powder

½ teaspoon paprika

½ teaspoon salt

2 teaspoons olive oil

4 pork chops

Fresh parsley, for garnish (optional)

EQUIPMENT

Baking sheet

Cooking spray

Gallon-size food storage bag

Tongs or fork

Meat thermometer

1. Preheat the oven to 425°F. Coat a baking sheet with nonstick cooking spray.

2. Combine the bread crumbs, Italian seasoning, garlic powder, onion powder, paprika, salt, and olive oil in a gallon-size food storage bag and shake until the ingredients are completely mixed.

3. One at a time, place the pork chops inside the bag and shake until the pork chops are completely covered. Place the pork chops on the baking sheet.

4. Bake for 25 minutes, turning the pork chops over with the tongs or fork halfway through, or until a meat thermometer registers 145°F.

5. Garnish with the parsley (if using).

FRENCH BREAD PIZZA

MAKES
4 servings
PREP TIME:
10 minutes
COOK TIME:
10 minutes

EGG
FREE

NUT
FREE

You have recipes for breakfast pizza and lunch pizza now at your fingertips, so it only makes sense to have one more pizza recipe designed for dinner. Add your favorite toppings to crusty French bread and you've got a filling meal that takes only minutes to make!

INGREDIENTS

1 loaf French bread

4 tablespoons butter, melted

½ teaspoon garlic powder

½ cup crumbled Italian sausage

½ cup pizza or marinara sauce

¼ teaspoon dried basil

¼ teaspoon dried oregano

1 cup shredded mozzarella cheese

¼ cup red onion slices

¼ cup red bell pepper slices

¼ cup yellow bell pepper slices

¼ cup green bell pepper slices

1 tablespoon olive oil

½ teaspoon red pepper flakes (optional)

EQUIPMENT

Baking sheet

Cooking spray

Knife

Small bowl

Pastry brush

Large skillet

Spoon

1. Preheat the oven to 400°F. Coat a baking sheet with nonstick cooking spray.

2. Slice the bread loaf in half, then cut each piece lengthwise. Place on the baking sheet, crust side down.

3. In a small bowl, mix the butter and garlic powder together. Use a pastry brush to spread the mixture onto the bread.

4. Bake for 5 minutes.

5. While the bread is baking, brown the sausage in a large skillet over medium heat. Set aside.

6. When the bread is ready, carefully remove from the oven. Spoon on the sauce, then sprinkle on the basil and oregano.

7. Add the mozzarella cheese, sausage, onion slices, and bell peppers. Drizzle the olive oil over the top.

8. Bake for 5 to 6 more minutes, or until the cheese is melted and bubbling.

9. Sprinkle with the red pepper flakes (if using) and enjoy.

Make It Your Way: Change up this recipe with your favorite toppings, from pepperoni to Buffalo chicken.

SUPERSTAR SNACKS

Savor the flavor of summer!

WATERMELON LEMONADE SLUSHY

MAKES
2 slushies

PREP TIME:
10 minutes

FREEZE TIME:
6 hours or
overnight

If you're looking for a cool snack for a hot day, it doesn't get much better than a slushy! Now you can skip the convenience-store run and make your own at home with a combination of two favorite summer flavors.

DAIRY FREE EGG FREE

GLUTEN FREE NUT FREE

VEGAN VEGE-TARIAN

INGREDIENTS

1½ cups lemonade

1½ cups cubed watermelon, divided

EQUIPMENT

Ice cube tray

Quart-size food storage bag

Blender

1. Pour the lemonade into 12 compartments of an ice cube tray and place in the freezer.

2. Put 1 cup of the watermelon into a quart-size food storage bag and place it in the freezer. Keep the remaining watermelon in the refrigerator.

3. Let the lemonade and watermelon freeze for at least 6 hours or overnight.

4. In a blender, whirl the frozen lemonade, frozen watermelon, and chilled watermelon on high for 1 to 2 minutes, or until the mixture becomes a slushy consistency.

Make It Your Way: Try substituting raspberries for watermelon to make a yummy raspberry lemonade slushy.

MARSHMALLOW TREAT FLOWERS

MAKES
4 flowers
PREP TIME:
10 minutes
COOK TIME:
15 minutes

Who knew flower arranging could be so delicious? With just three ingredients and a little food coloring, you can make a batch of edible blooms in minutes. The process may get a little messy, but that's part of what makes it so much fun.

INGREDIENTS

3 tablespoons unsalted butter, divided

1 package (10 ounces)
mini marshmallows, divided

2 choices of food coloring

6 cups crispy rice cereal, divided

EQUIPMENT

2 8 x 8-inch glass baking dishes

Cooking spray

Large saucepan

Wooden spoon

Flower-shaped cookie cutter

Round cookie cutter (smaller than the flower-shaped cutter)

1. Coat two 8 x 8-inch glass baking dishes with nonstick cooking spray.

2. In a large saucepan, melt 1½ tablespoons of the butter.

3. Stir in half of the marshmallows and continue to stir until completely melted. Add a few drops of one food coloring.

4. Add 3 cups of the cereal and stir until completely covered.

TIPS

These treats get sticky! If you want to avoid having them stick to you as you're molding them, just get your hands wet first.

5. Pour the cereal mixture into one of the glass dishes. Using the wooden spoon, spread the mixture to the sides.

6. Wash out the saucepan and repeat with the remaining butter, marshmallows, cereal, and second food coloring. Spread evenly in the second glass dish.

7. Once the treats have hardened (about 30 minutes), use a flower-shaped cookie cutter to cut two flower shapes from each color.

8. Next, cut circles out of the center of each flower with the round cookie cutter.

9. Switch them out so that each flower has an alternate-colored center. Gently push the edges of each flower's hole inward so that the center will attach to the new flower.

Make It Your Way: Use different shapes of cookie cutters to make your own marshmallow treat creations.

FRUITY TACOS

Don't limit your tortillas to meat and cheese! Fill them with a fun fruit fiesta and enjoy a sweet snack that everyone will rave about. The special cinnamon-sugar touch to the shells makes all the difference.

MAKES
6 tacos
PREP TIME:
10 minutes
COOK TIME:
5 minutes

EGG
FREE

VEGE-
TARIAN

INGREDIENTS

1 tablespoon granulated sugar

½ teaspoon cinnamon

6 5-inch flour tortillas

1 tablespoon unsalted butter, melted

½ peach, diced

¼ cup blueberries

½ cup blackberries

¼ cup hulled and sliced strawberries

¼ cup mandarin orange sections

2 tablespoons chopped walnuts

2 tablespoons honey

EQUIPMENT

Small bowl

Cutting board or parchment paper

Pastry brush

Oven-safe taco stand
or baking rack and pan

1. Preheat the oven to 375°F.

2. In a small bowl, combine the sugar and cinnamon. Set aside.

TIPS

You can make the tortillas ahead of time, but don't fill with the fruit until ready to serve or they'll become soggy.

3. Lay the tortillas flat on a cutting board or on parchment paper on the counter. Using a pastry brush and half of the melted butter, coat one side of each tortilla circle. Then using half of the sugar mixture, sprinkle it on each circle.

4. Flip the tortillas and repeat.

5. Place the tortillas in an oven-safe taco stand and bake for 5 minutes. If you don't have a taco stand, hang the tortillas over the bars of an oven rack and bake with a baking pan underneath.

6. Remove the tortillas from the oven and let cool for 5 minutes.

7. Fill the tortillas with the fruit, top with the nuts, and drizzle with the honey.

SWEET-AND-SALTY TRAIL MIX

MAKES
4 servings
PREP TIME:
5 minutes

EGG
FREE

Trail mix is the perfect snack for munching on the go. Have a little flavor fun by mixing up and enjoying this sweet-and-salty combination.

INGREDIENTS

½ cup salted peanuts

¼ cup dried cranberries

¼ cup chocolate candies or chocolate chips

½ cup mini marshmallows

EQUIPMENT

Large mixing bowl

Wooden spoon

1. In a large bowl, combine the peanuts, dried cranberries, chocolate candies or chips, and mini marshmallows.

2. Enjoy straight from the bowl or separate the trail mix into plastic snack bags.

Make It Your Way: Try using different ingredient combinations! Substitute raisins for the cranberries.

APPLE CHIPS

Introducing chips that are actually good for you! Plus, they're simple to make with ingredients you probably have on hand right now. You'll need to wait a bit before they're ready, but one taste will tell you the wait was totally worth it.

MAKES
8 servings
PREP TIME:
10 minutes
COOK TIME:
2½ hours
ADDITIONAL
TIME:
45 minutes

 DAIRY FREE
 EGG FREE
 GLUTEN FREE
 NUT FREE
 VEGAN
 VEGETARIAN

INGREDIENTS

2 large apples

1 tablespoon granulated sugar

1 teaspoon cinnamon

EQUIPMENT

Baking sheet

Parchment paper

Mandoline slicer or knife

Small bowl

1. Preheat the oven to 225°F. Line a baking sheet with parchment paper.

2. Using a mandoline, slice the apples on the thinnest setting. If you don't have a mandoline, slice the apples carefully and as thinly as possible with a knife.

3. Lay the apple slices on the parchment paper.

4. In a small bowl, combine the sugar and cinnamon.

5. Sprinkle the apple slices with half the sugar-cinnamon mixture. Flip over and sprinkle with the remaining sugar-cinnamon mixture.

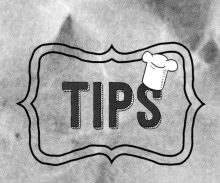

TIPS

The thinner your apple chips are, the crispier they will be.

If your chips are not as crispy as you'd like after the time is up, continue to bake them in 20-minute increments.

6. Bake for 90 minutes, then turn the slices over and bake for another hour.

7. Turn off the oven but leave the apple chips inside for 45 minutes more before removing the chips to enjoy.

Make It Your Way: You can make these apple chips sugar-free by sprinkling them with cinnamon only.

CHOCOLATE CHIP ENERGY BITES

MAKES
24 bites

PREP TIME:
10 minutes

COOK TIME:
1 hour

EGG FREE

VEGE-TARIAN

Filled with a yummy blend of peanut butter, coconut, and chocolate chips, these easy-to-make energy bites are fun (and just the right amount of messy) to mix and roll. Let them fuel your lunch box or after-school activities.

INGREDIENTS

2 cups old-fashioned oats

⅔ cup peanut butter

½ cup honey

½ cup coconut

½ cup chocolate chips

EQUIPMENT

Large mixing bowl

Wooden spoon

Airtight storage container

1. In a large bowl, combine the oats, peanut butter, honey, coconut, and chocolate chips.

2. Refrigerate the mixture for an hour.

3. Roll the mixture into bite-size balls.

4. Store in an airtight container in the refrigerator until ready to enjoy.

RAINBOW FRUIT SALAD

MAKES
6 servings
PREP TIME:
15 minutes

This colorful snack is both delicious and healthy, so that means it's definitely parent-approved. Follow the recipe exactly or customize with your own favorite fruits. It makes a great side to go with dinner or a fun party addition.

DAIRY FREE
EGG FREE
GLUTEN FREE
NUT FREE
VEGE-TARIAN

INGREDIENTS

½ cup strawberries, hulled and cut in half lengthwise

½ cup mandarin orange sections

½ cup pineapple chunks

½ cup kiwi chunks

½ cup seedless purple grapes

½ cup blueberries

3 tablespoons honey

½ tablespoon lime juice

EQUIPMENT

Large bowl or hollowed pineapple

Paring knife or strawberry huller

Small bowl

Spoon

1. In a large bowl or hollowed pineapple, layer or arrange the fruit for rainbow effect. (To hollow a pineapple, ask an adult for help.)

2. In a small bowl, mix the honey and lime juice together. Drizzle the mixture over the fruit.

CARAMEL POPCORN TREATS

MAKES
12 treats

PREP TIME:
10 minutes

COOK TIME:
5 minutes

EGG
FREE

Want a fun twist on caramel popcorn? You'll love making these popcorn squares. Filled with the sweet flavors of marshmallows, chocolate chips, and caramel, they make the perfect snack for movie night.

INGREDIENTS

1 regular-size bag (3.2 ounces) microwave popcorn, butter-flavored

2 tablespoons unsalted butter

3 cups mini marshmallows

¼ cup milk chocolate chips

⅓ cup caramel sauce

EQUIPMENT

Large saucepan

Wooden spoon

8 x 8-inch baking dish

Cooking spray

Spoon or squeeze bottle

Knife

1. Microwave the popcorn according to package directions. Set aside.

2. In a large saucepan over low heat, melt the butter.

3. Add the marshmallows, stirring frequently until completely melted.

4. Remove from the heat and stir in the popcorn to completely coat with marshmallow.

5. Spray an 8 x 8-inch baking dish with nonstick cooking spray, then add the popcorn mixture and spread evenly.

6. Sprinkle the chocolate chips over the top while the popcorn mixture is still warm.

7. Using a spoon or squeeze bottle, drizzle the caramel sauce over the top and let sit for a few minutes, until the caramel sets.

8. Cut into squares and serve.

Make It Your Way: Try using different flavors of marshmallows and chips beyond chocolate—peanut butter could be delish.

PEPPERONI PRETZELS

Why eat pretzels straight from the bag when you can do something fun with them instead? Turn your mini pretzels into crunchy little pizzas just by adding a few delicious toppings.

MAKES
4 servings
PREP TIME:
10 minutes
COOK TIME:
15 minutes

INGREDIENTS

18 (about 2 cups) mini pretzel twists

⅔ cup shredded mozzarella cheese

½ teaspoon red pepper flakes

18 pepperoni slices

EQUIPMENT

Baking sheet

Aluminum foil

1. Preheat the oven to 400°F. Line a baking sheet with aluminum foil.

2. Spread the mini pretzel twists on the foil in a single layer. Top with the mozzarella cheese, then sprinkle with the red pepper flakes. Add a pepperoni slice to each.

3. Bake for 15 minutes, or until the cheese is bubbling.

Make It Your Way: For another fun twist, try nacho pretzels topped with shredded cheddar cheese and salsa.

VERY BERRY ICE POPS

MAKES
6 ice pops
PREP TIME:
20 minutes
FREEZE TIME:
Overnight

These berry-filled frozen treats are so easy and refreshing, you'll never want store-bought ice pops again. Keep the freezer stocked because everyone in the family will be reaching for one!

DAIRY FREE · EGG FREE · GLUTEN FREE · NUT FREE · VEGAN · VEGETARIAN

INGREDIENTS

6 medium strawberries, hulled and cut into chunks

⅔ cup halved raspberries

½ cup blueberries

1½ cups apple juice

EQUIPMENT

Knife

6 ice pop molds

6 wooden craft sticks

1. Fill each of six ice pop molds with the fruit.

2. Add the apple juice, stopping about ½ inch from the top.

3. Insert a wooden craft stick into each mold. (The fruit should be thick enough to hold the stick in place.)

4. Freeze overnight.

> **Make It Your Way:** Try different fruits, such as blackberries, cherries, and even sliced bananas, and juices (grape is a great choice).

NACHO FRIES

Fast-food commercials piquing your snack appetite? Skip the drive-through and head to your kitchen. Piled high with all your favorite nacho ingredients, from beef to cheese, these fries are full of flavor and fun to share.

MAKES
4 servings
PREP TIME:
10 minutes
COOK TIME:
20 minutes

INGREDIENTS

1 bag (32 ounces) frozen french fries

½ cup 80 or 85% lean ground beef

½ package taco seasoning

⅓ cup water

¾ cup shredded cheddar cheese

½ cup diced tomatoes

¼ cup sliced or diced jalapeños (optional)

¼ cup sour cream

EQUIPMENT

Baking sheet

Large skillet

Wooden spoon or spatula

1. Preheat the oven according to package directions for the fries.

2. Spread the fries in a single layer on a baking sheet. Cook according to package directions, flipping the fries halfway through.

3. While the fries are baking, cook the ground beef in a large skillet over medium heat. Drain and return to the skillet.

4. Add the taco seasoning and water to the beef. Bring to a boil, then reduce the heat and simmer until the sauce thickens.

5. Top the cooked fries with the cheese and return to the oven just long enough for the cheese to melt, about 2 minutes.

6. Top with the cooked beef, tomatoes, and jalapeños (if using). Place a scoop of sour cream in the middle.

CREAM CHEESE APPLE RINGS

MAKES
8 slices
PREP TIME:
10 minutes

You can take apples from ordinary to all dressed up in just a few quick steps. Slice the fruit, add cream cheese and sweet toppings, and you've got a great after-school snack.

EGG FREE

NUT FREE

GLUTEN FREE

VEGE-TARIAN

INGREDIENTS

2 large apples

½ cup cream cheese

½ cup raisins

½ cup chocolate chips

EQUIPMENT

Cutting board

Apple corer

Chef's knife

Butter knife or small spatula, for spreading

1. Place an apple with the stem up on a cutting board. Press the apple corer down through the center of the apple. Pull the tool back out to remove the core. Repeat for the remaining apple.

2. Slice each apple into four rings.

3. Spread cream cheese over each ring, then top with the raisins and chocolate chips.

Make It Your Way: Try toppings such as caramel sauce with granola or nuts.

AWESOME DESSERTS

S'MORES BARK

When you can't build a campfire, you can still enjoy all the goodness of s'mores with this bark recipe! You'll be amazed how well the classic combination of ingredients comes together in a new, easy, indoor way.

MAKES
18 pieces

PREP TIME:
10 minutes

COOK TIME:
8-9 minutes

ADDITIONAL TIME:
30 minutes

EGG FREE

NUT FREE

INGREDIENTS

16 graham crackers

1 cup (2 sticks) unsalted butter

1 cup brown sugar

2 cups semisweet chocolate chips

1 cup mini marshmallows

EQUIPMENT

Baking sheet

Aluminum foil

Medium saucepan

Wooden spoon

Spatula

Plastic sandwich bag

Rolling pin

Knife

1. Preheat the oven to 400°F. Line a baking sheet with aluminum foil.

2. Set aside one graham cracker (to use for topping later). Spread the remaining graham crackers in a single layer on the foil.

3. In a medium saucepan over medium heat, combine the butter and brown sugar and bring to a boil. Boil for 2 minutes, stirring frequently.

4. Fold the whipped cream into the condensed milk and mix until well blended.

5. If using one food color, add it to the whipped cream mixture, mix well, and skip to step 8.

6. If using two food colors, separate the whipped cream mixture into two medium bowls, then add food coloring to each. Continue to step 7.

7. Pour half of the pink mixture into the chilled loaf pan, followed by half of the blue mixture. Repeat. Use a spatula to swirl them together gently. Be careful not to overmix or you'll lose the distinct pink and blue colors. Freeze for at least 6 hours. Continue to step 9.

8. Pour the mixture into the chilled loaf pan and freeze for at least 6 hours.

9. Scoop into bowls or ice cream cones and garnish with cotton candy (if using).

This sweet rainbow is guaranteed to bring smiles!

RAINBOW FUDGE

MAKES
12 squares

PREP TIME:
20 minutes

COOK TIME:
4 hours

Making fudge from scratch may sound tough, but you'll be amazed at just how easy it really is! This recipe uses just five ingredients and is so simple, you'll want to keep the ingredients on hand at all times to whip up a fudge surprise for friends or family.

EGG FREE

NUT FREE

GLUTEN FREE

VEGE-TARIAN

INGREDIENTS

3 cups white chocolate chips

1 can (14 ounces) sweetened condensed milk

2 tablespoons unsalted butter

1 teaspoon vanilla extract

Food coloring (at least four colors)

Rainbow sprinkles (optional)

EQUIPMENT

8 x 8-inch baking pan

Parchment paper

Medium saucepan

Large spoon

4 bowls

Spatula

Knife

1. Line an 8 x 8-inch baking pan with parchment paper.

2. In a medium saucepan, combine the white chocolate chips, condensed milk, and butter. Cook over medium heat, stirring frequently, until the chocolate is completely melted.

3. Stir in the vanilla.

4. Divide the fudge mixture equally into four bowls. (If using more food colors, increase the number of bowls.)

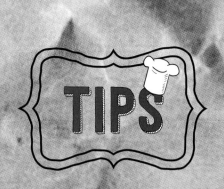

If you want your layers to be completely smooth and not blend into each other at all, divide the chocolate chip mixture into four bowls before melting. Melt one bowl of chocolate at a time, then layer and freeze for 10 minutes before melting and adding the next layer.

5. Pour one bowl of fudge into the pan and spread evenly across the bottom. One at a time, layer the remaining colors into the pan, spreading evenly after adding each color.

6. Refrigerate until solid enough to cut, about 4 hours. Top with the rainbow sprinkles (if using).

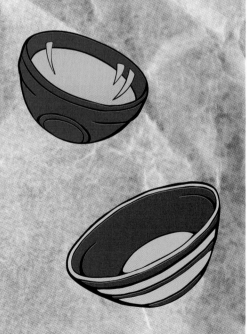

CHOCOLATE-PEANUT BUTTER COOKIES

MAKES
24 cookies

PREP TIME:
20 minutes

ADDITIONAL
TIME:
30 minutes

VEGE-
TARIAN

Peanut butter and chocolate are a match made in dessert heaven. Enjoy them together in these stuffed cookies that get a head start by using vanilla wafer cookies. Then you can devote more time to chocolate dipping and decorating—so much fun!

INGREDIENTS

12 tablespoons creamy peanut butter

48 vanilla wafer cookies

2 cups chocolate chips

¼ cup candy melts

Colored sprinkles (optional)

EQUIPMENT

Baking sheet

Parchment or wax paper

Spoon or spatula

2 small microwave-safe bowls

Fork

Small squeeze bottle

1. Line a baking sheet with parchment or wax paper.

2. Put ½ tablespoon of peanut butter on a wafer cookie. Top it with another wafer cookie and push together gently until the peanut butter just reaches the cookie edges. Repeat with the remaining cookies and peanut butter. Set aside.

3. Pour the chocolate chips into a small microwave-safe bowl and microwave for 1 minute. Stir. Continue to microwave and stir in 30-second increments until melted and smooth.

TIPS

An easy chocolate-dipping technique: Drop the cookie in the melted chocolate, flip it over with a fork, and use the fork to lift the cookie out. (Don't pierce the cookie with the fork; just place the fork under it.) Tap the fork lightly on the side of the bowl to help any excess chocolate drip off.

Add the sprinkles while the chocolate is still soft. Once the chocolate hardens, they'll roll off.

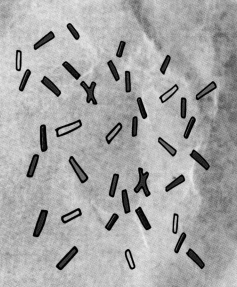

4. One at a time, dip the cookies in the chocolate. Let any excess chocolate drip off, then place the cookies on the lined baking sheet.

5. Place the candy melts in a small microwave-safe bowl and microwave for 30 seconds. Stir. Continue to microwave and stir in 30-second increments until melted and smooth.

6. Pour the melted candy melts into a squeeze bottle and drizzle over the cookies, or drizzle with a spoon instead.

7. Add the sprinkles (if using) and refrigerate for 30 minutes.

Make It Your Way: For seasonal cookies, dip in white chocolate and drizzle melted candy melts over the top. Use red and green for Christmas, pink and red for Valentine's Day, or red, white, and blue for the Fourth of July.

BLUEBERRY HAND PIES

These treats are called hand pies because you can ditch the silverware and just pick them up to take a bite of the flaky crust and fruity filling. Delish! They're super-casual to make too: cut the crust into any shape you like, stuff it with blueberries, and seal to bake.

MAKES
4 pies
PREP TIME:
10 minutes
COOK TIME:
10 minutes

NUT
FREE

VEGE-
TARIAN

INGREDIENTS

1 tablespoon all-purpose flour

2 refrigerated piecrusts (1 box)

½ cup blueberry pie filling

1 egg

1 tablespoon confectioners' sugar

EQUIPMENT

Large cutting board

5-inch cookie cutter

Baking sheet

Spoon

Fork

Knife

Small bowl

Pastry brush

Sifter

1. Preheat the oven to 425°F.

2. Sprinkle the flour onto a large cutting board and unroll one piecrust. Use a 5-inch cookie cutter to cut four shapes out of the piecrust.

3. Unroll the second piecrust and repeat.

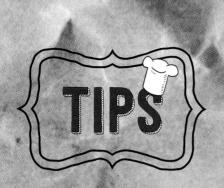

TIPS

If the piecrusts have been stored in the freezer, make sure they're completely thawed before you begin. Otherwise, they'll break apart when you unroll them.

4. Place four piecrusts on an ungreased baking sheet. Drop 2 tablespoons of pie filling into the center of each.

5. Top with the remaining piecrusts and seal by pushing a fork around the edges.

6. Cut a small X into the top of each crust.

7. In a small bowl, crack and beat the egg. Use a pastry brush to brush egg onto the top of each pie.

8. Bake for about 10 minutes, or until the piecrusts turn golden brown.

9. Let cool for about 5 minutes, then sprinkle with the confectioners' sugar.

Make It Your Way: Switch up this recipe by using apple or cherry filling instead.

CONFETTI CUPCAKE CONES

MAKES
12 cones
PREP TIME:
20 minutes
COOK TIME:
12-15 minutes

It's the best of both worlds: ice cream cones and cupcakes!
These pretty confetti cupcake cones are perfect for parties.

CONE CAKES INGREDIENTS

12 sugar cones

1 box confetti cake mix

1¼ cups water*

3 eggs*

½ cup vegetable oil*

1 cup white candy melts

Colored sprinkles

BUTTERCREAM FROSTING INGREDIENTS

1 cup salted butter, softened

1 teaspoon vanilla extract

4 cups confectioners' sugar

2 tablespoons heavy whipping cream

* *These are the ingredients listed on most boxes of cake mix. If your mix calls for different ingredients, use those instead.*

EQUIPMENT

Cupcake cone baking rack

Hand or stand mixer

2 large mixing bowls

Toothpick

Small microwave-safe bowl

Decorating bag with tip

1. Preheat the oven to 350°F. Place the cones in a cupcake cone baking rack.

2. **To make the cone cakes:** Using a hand or stand mixer, combine the cake mix, water, eggs, and vegetable oil in a large bowl.

TIPS

If you don't have a cupcake cone baking rack, use flat-bottom cake cones and stand them upright in a muffin tin for baking. Have an adult help you carefully lift them into and out of the oven. Add a few minutes of baking time if you're using this kind of cone.

3. Fill the cones to about an inch from the top with cake batter. Bake for 12 to 15 minutes, or until a toothpick inserted into the cake comes out clean. Set the cone cakes aside to cool.

4. When the cupcakes are cool, place the candy melts in a small microwave-safe bowl. Microwave in 30-second increments, stirring after each, until the chocolate is melted and smooth.

5. Roll the rims of the ice cream cones in the chocolate, cover with sprinkles, and return to the baking rack.

6. **To make the frosting:** In a large bowl, beat the butter and vanilla until smooth.

7. Add the confectioners' sugar, a little at a time. Mix in the whipping cream until the buttercream is the desired consistency.

8. Place the frosting in a decorating bag and top each dessert with frosting and sprinkles.

Introducing everyone's new favorite birthday treat!

Make dessert magical with colorful creations!

MINI UNICORN CHEESECAKES

MAKES
12 mini
cheesecakes
PREP TIME:
30 minutes
FREEZE TIME:
30 minutes

EGG FREE

NUT FREE

These unicorn cheesecakes are almost too pretty to eat...but we're guessing that won't stop anyone! Have a blast whipping up the luscious cheesecake, adding some fun colors, and decorating with flair.

GRAHAM CRACKER CRUST INGREDIENTS

6 graham crackers

2½ tablespoons granulated sugar

3 tablespoons unsalted butter, melted

CHEESECAKE INGREDIENTS

8 ounces cream cheese

½ cup granulated sugar

1½ tablespoons vanilla extract

¾ cup heavy whipping cream

4 colors of food coloring (suggested: pink, green, yellow, and blue)

DECORATIONS INGREDIENTS

Black decorating gel

12 horn-shaped snacks

3 packages (0.33 ounces each) candy flowers

EQUIPMENT

Plastic sandwich bag

Rolling pin

Medium mixing bowl

Mini cheesecake pan (with removable bottoms)

Large mixing bowl or stand mixer bowl

Stand or hand mixer

Beater attachment

Whisk attachment

Wooden spoon

4 small bowls

1. **To make the graham cracker crust:** Place graham crackers in a plastic sandwich bag and use a rolling pin to crush them. Make sure there are no large chunks remaining.

2. In a medium bowl, mix the graham cracker crumbs, sugar, and butter.

3. Check that each section of the mini cheesecake pan has the bottom pieces inserted, then spoon an equal amount of graham cracker mixture into each. Using one of the extra bottom inserts or your fingers, press down firmly until the mixture is compact. Set aside.

4. **To make the cheesecake:** In a large bowl or stand mixer bowl, use the beater attachment of the mixer to beat the cream cheese, sugar, and vanilla until well blended. If using the stand mixer bowl, transfer to another bowl. Set aside.

5. Using the whisk attachment, whisk the whipping cream until firm peaks begin to form. (If your mixer doesn't have a whisk attachment, use the regular beaters instead.)

6. Fold the whipping cream into the cheesecake mixture.

7. Divide the cheesecake mixture into four small bowls. Add a different color of food coloring to each one.

8. Layer the cheesecake colors into the pan sections. If the mixture is too thick to layer, stir for another minute to soften it.

9. Place the pan in the freezer for approximately 30 minutes, or until the cheesecakes harden.

10. Remove the cheesecakes from the pan by pushing each one up from the bottom.

11. **To decorate the cheesecakes:** Use black decorating gel to make the eyes. Add a horn and six to eight candy flowers to each, and refrigerate until ready to serve.

Make It Your Way: Switch it up and use neon food coloring for brighter unicorns.

TIPS

Cheesecake can be frozen for up to a month. You can add the eyes before freezing, then add the horns and flowers when you're ready to serve.

You may want to practice making a set of eyes before decorating your unicorn. If the decorating gel comes out too thick, put some in an icing bag and cut the tip slightly (you can substitute a plastic sandwich bag if you don't have icing bags). How much you cut will determine the thickness of the gel. Start with a very small cut and go from there.

MARSHMALLOW POPS

MAKES
6 pops
PREP TIME:
15 minutes
ADDITIONAL
TIME:
10 minutes

With marshmallows, colorful candy melt, and rainbow sprinkles, these pops take just minutes to make but add bright fun to the dessert tray. Even sweeter, you can customize them any way you want: use team colors or create a party theme.

INGREDIENTS

24 regular-size marshmallows

½ cup each of orange, blue, and pink candy melts

Rainbow sprinkles

EQUIPMENT

Baking sheet

Wax paper

6 candy sticks

3 microwave-safe bowls

Spoon

Squeeze bottle or spoon for drizzling

1. Line a baking sheet with wax paper.

2. Push each of the candy sticks through four marshmallows. Set aside.

3. Pour the candy melts into separate microwave-safe bowls. Melt one color for a minute, then stir. Continue to heat in 30-second increments, stirring each time, until the candy is melted and smooth.

4. Holding the sticks over the bowl one at a time, spoon candy melt over two sticks of marshmallows and lay on the baking sheet.

TIPS

If your candy is too thick, even when melted, stir in vegetable oil a teaspoon at a time until you get a consistency that works.

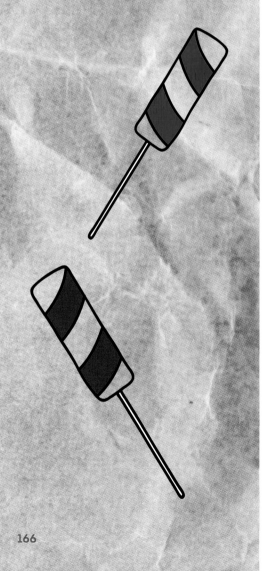

5. Repeat steps 3 and 4, covering two sticks of marshmallows per color.

6. Using a squeeze bottle or a spoon, drizzle the remaining candy in alternating colors over the marshmallows. Scatter the rainbow sprinkles over the candy.

7. Refrigerate for 10 minutes, or until the coating sets.

Make It Your Way: Choose colors coordinated with an upcoming holiday, like pink and red for Valentine's Day.

CHOCOLATE MOUSSE BITES

MAKES
15 bites
PREP TIME:
20 minutes

This melt-in-your-mouth dessert is so delish that it disappears almost as soon as you set it on the table. It only looks fancy—it's actually pretty simple to make with just five ingredients and five steps!

INGREDIENTS

2 ounces sweet baking chocolate

2 ounces semisweet chocolate

1 cup heavy whipping cream

¼ cup confectioners' sugar, sifted

1 box (15 count) phyllo shells

EQUIPMENT

Medium microwave-safe bowl

Wooden spoon or spatula

Medium mixing bowl

Stand or hand mixer

Sifter

Decorating bag with tip

1. In a medium microwave-safe bowl, combine the sweet and semisweet chocolate. Melt in the microwave at 50 percent power in 30-second increments, stirring each time, until the chocolate is melted and smooth. Set aside.

2. In a separate medium bowl, beat the whipping cream at medium speed until it begins to froth.

3. Gradually add the confectioners' sugar and beat until soft peaks form.

TIPS

Sifting the confectioners' sugar first will give the chocolate mousse a smoother texture.

4. Gently fold the whipped cream into the chocolate.

5. Fill a decorating bag with the chocolate mousse mixture and squeeze into the phyllo shells.

Make It Your Way: Decorate the phyllo shells by dipping them in chocolate, then adding sprinkles.

CHOCOLATE PRETZELS WITH CARAMEL

MAKES
6 servings
(½ cup each)

PREP TIME:
15 minutes

ADDITIONAL
TIME:
10 minutes

This may be one of the easiest desserts ever! Toss chocolate and caramel over pretzels, add a few nuts, and you've got a delicious combination of salty and sweet.

INGREDIENTS

½ cup chocolate chips

2 cups mini pretzels

¼ cup caramel sauce

¼ cup chopped walnuts

EQUIPMENT

Baking sheet

Wax paper

Small microwave-safe bowl

Wooden spoon

1. Line a baking sheet with wax paper.

2. Place the chocolate chips in a small microwave-safe bowl and microwave for 30 seconds. Stir. Continue to microwave and stir in 30-second increments until the chocolate is melted and smooth.

3. Fold the pretzels into the chocolate and stir gently until they are completely covered. Pour into a single layer on the wax paper.

4. Drizzle the caramel sauce over the pretzels, then top with the chopped nuts.

5. Refrigerate for 10 minutes, or until the chocolate has set.

ORANGE CREAMSICLE MILKSHAKE

MAKES
2 milkshakes
PREP TIME:
5 minutes

EGG FREE

GLUTEN FREE

NUT FREE

Orange you glad you can whip up this perfect Creamsicle in a glass in just 5 minutes? The ingredients are easy to keep on hand for whenever a shake calls.

INGREDIENTS

¾ cup orange soda

⅔ cup (2 scoops) vanilla ice cream

⅔ cup (2 scoops) orange sherbet

Whipped cream for topping

Orange slices and cherries,
for garnish (optional)

EQUIPMENT

Blender

Ice cream scoop

2 glasses

1. Pour the orange soda into a blender.

2. Add the vanilla ice cream and orange sherbet. Blend until creamy.

3. Pour into two glasses and top with whipped cream. Garnish with the orange slices and cherries (if using).

INDEX

ROLL IT, SLICE IT, MASH IT, DICE IT!